ALL PIECES OF A LEGACY

CHARLES ENTREKIN

BERKELEY POETS WORKSHOP & PRESS

Some of the material in this book appeared previously in the
following publications: *Southern Poetry Review, Green Horse For
Poetry, US1 Worksheets, Eternity SF, Berkeley Poets Cooperative.*

This book was funded in part by a grant from the National
Endowment for the Arts.

Cover design and artwork: Maggie Entrekin.

For Demian, Caleb, and Maggie

CONTENTS

Moments   (poetry)

    Here In The Dark, Love

    Birmingham

    Alabama Kudzu

    Let's Play A Game

    Ballad

    Dink

    Parting

    Reducing Everything After Leaving

    In San Francisco

    Awakening

    Montana

    On Your Birthday

    Missoula Spring

    Earthsong

    All Pieces Of A Legacy

    Easter Triptych

Voices   (fiction)

    A Darker Room

    Palace Of New Beginnings

    Hamburgers

    Apples

MOMENTS

I'm out here in the dark, love,
because I wanted to be alone.
Because I wanted something to give-in to.
I tried to remember how lives change, always
altered and yet remain the same, but tonight
  I felt something break
as after a long fall. Now even our names
seem best left alone, unchanged
like names buried character by character
in stone.
  I remember the tunes, love,
that's why I've come. I remember
the honeysuckle touch of your tongue.
  You can see I'm here without my clothes,
and the moon's not bright; but listen to me first,
something's gone wrong in my life, some
things I've not told you about. Listen.
Some blood always runs cold as mine.
This nakedness on the lawn
contains all I've ever been.
  I know you're going to say
I keep bringing you what has changed
without me.
  I know when I wake
in the morning my seed will remain
one more secret egg on your plate,
but you see I don't care, I also
will not know what's become of us.

BIRMINGHAM

Of all the places you could die
trapped if you didn't leave fast
or have lots of money, this is the one
you remember best. This is your birthplace.
    You wanted out the day she ran away,
left you the child and the furniture.
But you stayed, innocent and twenty-one,
made love to practiced women. One,
forty-one, who kept your child for free;
one, thirty-three, who hoped her husband
died, a little at a time; and one,
twenty-nine, who came to you animalized,
hardened with lies.
    It was a steel time town, younger
and harder than Birmingham Sunday could break.
Three black children died. You made love
to the wife of a salesman. He failed
to give her children. And failed again
she cried when you stopped cold,
told her, no, no more children.
    That night outside Memphis, the Mississippi
mosquitoes like furies bidding you goodbye,
you turn in your mind the meaning of escape.
Almost, you wanted to lie, you're innocent
if you don't go back. The child asleep, your red car
packed, you douse the fire and drive out fast.

ALABAMA KUDZU

This is the fear, the words
trapped in the back of your throat,
that nothing is enough.
    In your blood you trace
the inner latticework of kudzu,
you understand the brown trees,
all motion pulled to the ground,
like horses drowned in quicksand,
the tall and crumbling pine
beneath an undying green.
    But this is only the fear,
you have told yourself, regret nothing.
Your eyes are still blue, and inside
you are still capable of surrendering.

LET'S PLAY A GAME
[from a story told of my grandfather]

Say it was pretend, with a friend, around
1890 or 1910, and you've just come home
wearing your flannel shirt that's wet along
the cross of suspenders on your back.
Your eyes are wide with shock.
It was to be playing you were Jesse James
with your one shot squirrel gun, and you've run
all the way home, leaving behind the sloping hill,
the thick grotto of trees growing up at an angle
to your sense of balance, the one lone oak,
    leaving behind all those twisted dogwoods,
those Christ crooked trees bursting green and white
and the oak with your rope tied just as it was
supposed to be, that grass brown rope
that was your birthday present
    around his neck so blue and bent,
hanging from the tree you'd decided was the hanging tree.

He would be in the forest lifting out
his band-aid box, sandpaper glued to the bottom,
never carried a lighter, and the match would flare:
    the smell of pipe tobacco in the cold winter
air, and I remember him always working, planting,
fishing, walking: a man who distrusted words,
loved his dogs, who would be gone
    hunting all day with his dogs, listening
for the closing of the circle, to his best dog,
listening, leaning with his back against the mossed side,
against some dead old oak.

[*for my Uncle Bud*]

DINK

I know a man who, at birth,
was broken by a doctor whose hands
faltered in the too long and too hard delivery.
    He grew up broken, his eyes crossed,
his legs withered, his head too large in circumference,
and his whole back scarred from neck to hip.
    He was given one year, two, ten, and now he's thirty,
cousin Dink, with a grade school education,
without bitterness, with scars on his too often burned legs
that have no feeling, and
        would I send him a drinking glass,
the kind you buy at tourist spots, or if not that,
perhaps a road map of California?

My father paced me as we shovelled
until I grew tired and watched him
watching me
shovelling
and then when I stopped
he grinned
his feet sinking slowly in the loose dirt
the sweat pouring down his muscled back
in streams.
Somehow he won then
and even as I packed my bags
our angry eyes clashing like iron
and I turned my back on him
I felt that smile
as he shovelled on
past all endurance
that strength of his arms and back
that unworded smile of his disappointment.

REDUCING EVERYTHING AFTER LEAVING

If I told you I did not go thru that day, Dad,
that instead
the mirror of it hangs like an afterimage
on her low ceilings
                    blooming blood plants . . . .
Eidetic luxuriant preparation,
dying.
Her hands are shaking,
skinny blue hands, fingers
shaking.
Her Quaker heritage is calling,
her inner ears distorting the sounds.
That's how the dishes were broken in the first place.
I took one look
and time stopped in her stooping,
face pleading,
flesh river long and flat and winding
thru my birth and all my brothers after me.

Coming towards me
like light from a distant star
not yet arrived anywhere
he entered the park
fondling an animal-headed
smooth-carved redwood cane;
    then pushing his black
leather jacket loose at the neck
his dark-skinned hand
found and placed the harp,
the black eyes closing,
the coffined chords
a hymn, a dirge,
    and suddenly I know how
the sounds of what I have broken
are healing in the ground.

AWAKENING

I can hear the corners of my room touching,
The whole enclosed space leaning around and over me.
I am sealed inside, comfortable and warm, but
I have been out walking;
My hair is still damp with rain
And there is the feel of nearby fog
Moving around my feet.
My wool hat smells like a dead animal.

The dream of an ashen faced woman wakes me
and it's snowing
and I'm cold.

Her face is hidden
somewhere in shadows,
a phone booth
with one light on
that blinks once
and goes out.

In the dark
the refrigerator cuts on.
I listen to its whine,
the snow falling.

ON YOUR BIRTHDAY

I mark it down on my
calendar memory this
Thanksgiving on your
birthday and no presents
except Pat's hand-made
tray of recipes;
    and as it grows dark
outside with snow on the
ground all around us the
turkey cooking and the
football game
    I feel suddenly like a
stranger divided between
day and night, who's come
dressed against the cold in
an old shirt, old and full
of holes like a memory,
    and as if I've left my
body drifting in the dark
my hands in you struggle,
relax, and begin slowly to
move again these days like
petals blown before a wind.

for Maggie, in Montana, 1973

I have become
one of my own poems.
This morning
the covered streets
opened black
in melting snow.
I was wrong.
Winter gone, a flower
opens in me, a song, words
crawl in my veins,
a carnation of the brain,
a dogwood.

EARTHSONG

And what could she say
who knew it best, took nothing
kept nothing and gave no warning
she would stop and turn away.
No one knows how it happens
these roads stretch out through
snow, flare, and turn to covered
hills, trees quiet as cows
gathered for night.
No insects hum. An old barn
cracks from the cold. Every night
her old body hides in the dark
under the rustle of corn leaves.
I want to reach out
pull the land away
reach down and hold her
shining like moon on the snow.

ALL PIECES OF A LEGACY

You receive the memories, the hunger,
and the dreams shiny as the eyes of madmen
before stately antebellum mansions,
even for the poor more than they were,
like lightning bugs stuck to a summer evening.

Patterns like footprints in the grass
of a barefooted run with June bug
on a string, like a child hugged in the arms
of motherhood, tied to a solid, hard-backed green,
the buzzing, broken as first sex in the back of a car.

And you remember the funny talk of poontang
in barber shops before the hunt begins,
the talk of the remorseless chicken thief,
the hungry coon sought after in the night
out beyond the chinaberry tree, the mimosa
and crepe myrtle, out beyond even the dogwood

through the kudzu, hunted and smiling
from the pine tree, smiling at the dogs
pulled with chains from the moon-cut pine;
you remember that trapped and smiling, high-up coon,
you remember the hunger that would not cease, cease.

Not because on the screen on the right one woman fondles another woman's breast, brown round tit—it was without sound and anyhow not the one we paid to see—or because on the screen on the left the "Five Fingers of Death" played out a constant comic book mimicry of a movie; or even because of the one in the center, the one we paid to see, loud speaker on, mafia Godfather whisper, "My name is Vito Corleone," before he stabs and cuts from right to left, from navel to tit, into the fat man's sleep.

But because, for no reason, I've got a hard-on that won't go down, my wife sleeps on my shoulder, and my two kids have become, truly, progeny, as in extensions, and all of us are adrift at the auto movies.

And later, after the moral is announced—"The snack bar is closing."—on the highway home, I imagine the car coming up fast behind us is filled with Zebra killers, San Francisco variety, who don't care who they kill. And it comes to me, we are all trapped in a world-wide holy war, another one, destined to last one hundred years. The blood of Jesus is upon us. Holy Mother, holy Father. The racial unconscious carries only the vague outline of a mushroom, like a snapshot in the back pocket of America. The car passes us, a beat-up white buick. It touches the railing. A stream of sparks, single file, like metal tears.

VOICES

A DARKER ROOM

I

Time To Remember

Mama Newton was wearing her ankle-length black dress, dressed for town. She had said goodbye to her husband, but now she hesitated as if she might retrace her steps back to his chair. She stood in the shade under the eaves of their house and half-lifted her hand to wave, but he was not watching. He was looking out over the city toward Red Mountain. Her hand came back to her side. She turned, walked down the grass driveway, and was gone.

It was the first day he had been left alone. He was sitting in the backyard, his head and chest still swathed in bandages, catching the sunlight beside the fishpond. He watched the sun bleed toward the west, the industrial haze low over the valley. His eyes wandered over his backyard, convalescent, seeing and yet not seeing: the stump beside the garage that had been a fig tree, the rotted-out oak that had cast deep shadows over a green yard, his black buick sedan crumpled like something beaten and muti-lated, sitting there like a display of things gone wrong—*that anyone could have been in it and survived.* He stared and the bright silver holes seemed to spin out from the front fender.

He leaned back and noticed it the moment he looked: the garage, a whole section of the tin roof had not been nailed down properly; it would blow loose with the first heavy storm. He sat for what seemed a long time and stared at it. His mind wandered.

He remembered his father. It was the day of the funeral, a few days after his mother had died. His father had insisted he go, but he had refused. He wanted his mother alive. He had run to the barn to escape, but his father had come after him. Even now, like something fixed inside him, he watched his father come down from the house still wearing his straw hat. It had seemed such an odd thing, his wearing the straw hat with his black suit, those eyes so much like his own, saying, I'll deal with you later. They had not said a single word to each other. Had only stared. He remembered how finally his father had turned and walked stiffly upright back to the house. He had hated his father that day and, his disobedience burning inside, he had thrown himself through the crib's doorway into the thick darkness of leather and grain, the gloom of wasp nests, sinking into a wretchedness that would not be healed. Before dawn of the next day he had run away. He had never returned. His father had disowned him.

His eyes came back to the roof. He looked away, pained. A breeze carrying the scent of rain passed over him. He turned and stared. Then his 62-year-old washed-out face flushed red with the thought of it. He would repair it himself. He stood up on shaky legs and waited for the dizzy spell to pass before he entered the darkened garage and returned with the hammer and nails. His legs were trembling as he positioned the ladder and put one foot up. Then he climbed one step at a time, one foot in front of the other, holding on in long unsteady pauses to let the air into his damaged lungs, but going on stubbornly, his will to do for himself pushing him up and up until his old body could rest at the top. Then it passed over him as a shock that he had left the nails on the ground, all that effort, useless without the nails on the ground. He considered giving up, going back down, asking someone to do it for him, but, no, he could do for himself. He placed the hammer on the hot tin surface, pulled himself together and began the long climb down, his legs and hands shaking, each step an effort, all the strength of his will.

Once down he stared at the sack of nails with the pain, the foreknowledge of the nausea that would come with the bending over. Again, hesitation held him suspended between giving up and finishing the job; and even as he hesitated the struggle ended. The shaking of the ladder, the vibrations of his trembling, the hammer slipping closer and closer to the edge, and then hanging suspended between gravity and friction until it tilted over and fell.

When it struck the back of his head, the old legs gave up their strength at once, and he fell there beside the ladder, beside the hammer, the blood drying a dark stain on the ground.

II

Survival

Papa Newton rose up on one elbow and looked around. The room seemed familiar somehow. The thick smell of honeysuckle drifted through the open window. He felt too hot and threw back the covers. He had been sweating and was wet through and through. His long-johns clung to him, cloying, disturbing. Across the room an old woman was sleeping. (She was his wife, but he did not recognize her.) He climbed out of his bed and stood up. The room became a blur and he sat back down. He stared across the darkened room at the old woman. She looked familiar, his aunt maybe, his father's sister. No, it was someone else. He remembered a death, his father in black, bent over in the late afternoon sun, a single file procession of people moving like shadows over the ridge into the cemetery. He forgot it and stood up again. His legs trembled under him and he willed them to stop trembling. At first they would not obey him. He clenched his hands into fists. Began walking. And slowly the legs worked the way he wanted. He knew this house. He made it to the bathroom without a search. As he undressed, his body seemed constantly on the verge of betraying him. He fought to make his movements precise. The steam poured around him and he stared down into the tub. Had he turned the water on? He reached a hand up to his head and felt the thick bandages. He started to rip them away, but the contact of his hand pushed a blackness across his mind and he forgot everything except his pain. He found himself sitting on the bathroom floor listening to the water gush from the faucets. He was naked, his body wet and slippery on the bathroom tile. He felt a terrible need to get out of there and pulled himself to his feet, groped his way toward the door.

Leaning back against the closed door he felt safe. He bent

forward and breathed heavily. Then abruptly he straightened up and listened. Behind him, the sound of running water spilling onto the floor. A sudden fear went through him. He had to get out of there. He had to get back home. The screen door swished softly behind him as he waded out into the moonlight. Somehow he knew which way he was going and he didn't question it. He was going home. In his mind he was running.

The damp grass still cool on his bare feet, he stopped at a backyard gate and stared up at a huge full moon. He felt much better now. He knew what he had to do. And yet there was something that worried him. A face kept coming to him, soft and blurred, and then angry, scowling. In the distance a train whistled. And he was moving again, down the alley, dim lights lighting the sky off to his right, bent over and awkward, a naked pale white thing in the dark.

Small stones and pieces of glass cut at his feet. From time to time he wondered what had become of his shoes, but he did not stop or look down. He moved slowly, from alley to alley, moving south, ever inward toward the streets of downtown Birmingham. He passed the one-square-block of Jewish cemetery, and then he was stopped. A well-lit intersection to cross. The moon was high and small, behind him now. He stood in the shadows and listened. Car lights loomed up and whipped past. Footsteps were approaching. He hesitated, unsure of himself, and then he was running, a great awkward crane struggling to hurry, suddenly white-framed in oncoming lights, and then the haven of another alleyway.

He fell back against a building and nearly collapsed. He was exhausted. The air he breathed tasted like ash. He wanted to lie down and sleep. He knew his feet were ripped and bleeding, but he could barely feel them. Sleep, if only he could sleep, but something was building in him again. He moved forward, haltingly, a slow motion wraith stumbling from shadow to shadow. Again, a train called from the dark, and he knew he could not stop. He had to get to the railroad. He knew which freight to catch. He had to get home. Already he could see it, his father's house, the orchard trees around it, the hillside pasture, the high gray barn, and there was the path that would take him to them. His brothers and sisters would be waiting. His mother: HE COULD ALMOST FEEL HER ARMS AROUND HIM. And there would be the chores he had left undone. He would have to catch up. He would fix that leak in the barn. He would make it all up. It would be as if he had never left . . . .

He entered a shop-filled street in a trance. An apparition (his reflection) moved in the windows beside him. The street lamps flickered above. And then he saw it. It came from his left, something white, quick and flat. He stopped and turned. Stared. *It was a naked old man.* Moved towards it. And suddenly it reached for him, the mouth opening, toothless, and it screamed, a sound like choking, the bandaged head rearing, the wild owl eyes closing over him. His arms flailed, the ancient body burning red and stretching out for him, the hammer blows, the deafening hammer blows. He twisted, fighting for air, for release, the withered legs and genitals, and sinking to his knees, it let him go. He lay there in the center of light from the street lamp, and then his hands moved up over his face, his legs twisted under him, and a cry began, a palsied wail against the fear that was shaking him, a wail that had no beginning or end, that rose and fell like a flashing red light, like a siren in the darkness that closed over him.

III

Reprieve

The old woman held his hand as they turned off the highway onto the dirt road. There was something about her that he dimly recognized and accepted as her right to touch him. He allowed her to care for him. She reminded him of someone. He wasn't sure of whom, but it didn't make any difference. Something more important worked inside him constantly, something he had left undone, a face, someone who needed him. He leaned back and sweat ran under his shirt. The windows were rolled up to avoid the dust

29

roiling over the car. It rose and then fell over the thick, brown-covered pines and underbrush. The car moved as through a tunnel. His round white head rolled back, his eyes closed, and his face moved again with the struggle that slowly was claiming him, slowly, in the dark, in his dream of a naked old man reaching out to take him; and somehow, each time he woke, he knew he had only narrowly escaped.

He jerked awake. Outside there were flat wide fields of dust-covered cotton plants; and then at the edge of a green-thick, vine-covered mat of trees, he could see a sorghum mill: a mule moving in a predescribed circle, two men in straw hats, a heavy black smoke rising abruptly into a blue sky. Then they turned left and *he remembered*. That left turn. They had entered *his* road. This was his property. He owned it. He sat erect and looked around. This was all his, *his* farm. He jerked around and stared at the old woman beside him, but her face betrayed no emotion whatsoever, as calm as bone. He started away.

The house rose up on square-built brick legs, black, the faded tar paper revealing the boards beneath, the tin roof weathered to a dull gray. Papa Newton accepted the sight of it like a trunk of old and familiar clothes. There was a complete row of yellow tulips in front of the house, ringing the porch; and there was his rocking chair, still there, and the path across the culvert down to the barn. A broad sense of peace began to settle over him. It was like he had been away and come back, and though he couldn't remember from where, he didn't care. This was *his* house. Immediately he wanted to go inside and assume possession.

#

There would be no electricity. He wouldn't allow it. And the yellowed wallpaper would continue its slow fall from the corners of the ceiling, but, for a time, there would be evenings, the kerosine lanterns casting wide circles of light, alive with moths and mosquitoes, and the hard-shelled beetles clinging to the backs of screens. Papa would read again a week-old paper he had already read several times. Mama would be churning the milk from their two cows. And, for a time, there would be her strong even rhythm of hand and wood, and her seeming tireless strength to manage the days they had come to live again.

30

IV

Demands of the Body

Dawn, and in this September morning he watched the mists swirl thickly the length of his creek, the earth spongy and dark. He had walked the muddied path to the water's edge and then moved like a specter through the mist toward the pasture and his bottom land. In the quiet now he could hear the occasional flat tone of the cow's bell. He walked without hurry, and with his staff, a thick dried vine he had cut for himself, he poked at the rotted timbers as he passed.

He stopped where an old logging bridge had stood. It lay collapsed and sinking under the water. The water was high, backed up, bloated with swill. The creek seemed to flow in reverse, and brown, sawdust colored froth gathered and circled on the surface. He turned and started around the flooded muddy ground when a cottonmouth slipped from a limb off to his left. The hushed wet slap of its body went over him like a chill. He stood for a moment and stared, the off-yellow shading visible across its throat, and then he stepped over a deadfall and blocked its path to the water. A log on either side, the moccasin backed, then stopped and coiled. There was a hollow snapping noise. The mouth gaped open displaying the white gullet. He stabbed at it with his staff and laughed, but no sound issued from his throat.

When the snake lurched forward the old man almost lost his footing as he stepped to one side, his staff crashing down on the tail, the snake writhing in a mass that abruptly disappeared down the bank into the water. The old man stared. Nothing. The rings widened across the surface, bent, and then broke beneath the foam. Suddenly he was gasping. He could not get his breath. He staggered away from the water into a hollow of thorns and scrub and leaned back against a mossed-over oak. A heavy chest pain surged through him till he stood locked and rigid, his eyes glazed and staring out through the rising mist at a pale white sun hanging like something frozen that was melting inside him.

31

He rose from the ground and left the creek behind. Gradually the scrub turned to pine and he was walking on a path that moved parallel to the road. After a half-mile there was a place where only pasture grass separated him from the road. He gathered burdock in his socks as he cut left away from the path. He crossed the barbed wire fence where a top strand was broken. Then he stopped and looked up for the house. The brown chert road curved at a quarter of a mile and there it was, black and closed against the high rained-out gray. Off to the right he could see swatches of sunlight and already he could feel the heat rising as in a greenhouse.

He pulled his hat down tight and started out. The brim covered his eyes. His clothes were wet. They clung to him as he walked, drying to a wrinkled stiffness in the slight wind. In his mind there was no sense of the passage of time. He was leaning forward from the waist as if he were being pulled. And when he stumbled his pace quickened, his dignity preserved by momentum. His breath came harsh, a cold fire igniting in the exchange of air in his throat.

When he crossed the culvert and turned toward the house, he reared. Studied it. It was black and abandoned-looking. The porch posts were reinforced with two-by-fours nailed at crazy angles into the floor. He had forgotten his doing it. Concrete blocks were stacked together for steps; they tilted precariously apart. Why had it been allowed to happen? He was almost running when he reached the steps, spilled over them and fell cursing to the floor. He was on his feet faster than his age would seem to have allowed. He heaved at the door. His father's face washed over him like shame. He jerked harder. It refused him. He began to back up, his hands lifting, waving in the air like animals suddenly turned loose. He spun around, reached up, grabbed his wet-stained gray felt hat and threw it to the floor. Began jumping on it. Stomping at it. A wildness taking him over, his hands waving, the thin white strands of his hair whipping at his reddened face. He stopped abruptly. Picked up the crumpled hat. Threw it into the yard. Turned toward his staff still lying where it had fallen on the floor. As he bent over his eyes became fixed, his face masked with urgency. A long stitch-marked scar was visibly pink along the upper side of his bare white head.

The twisted thick-gnarled handle of his walking staff curved through the glass. She said nothing but stood there and stared at him, watched him pass through the unlit living room into the darker room which served as their bedroom. And still she did not move, but stood as if transfixed by some inner knowledge which held her dumb and rooted to the floor.

#

Inside and the door closed behind him, the soft curtained blackness assailed him with a quilted feeling that was close to suffocation. Each breath dragged a length of barbed wire down his throat. He was worried. The old woman was a mystery to him. He was afraid of her. When he had seen her something had risen in him dark and foreboding, opened like a wound that would not heal, like a grave, soft, the heavy sadness of a face that had wanted to comfort him, that bent toward him smelling of incense, of, *of his mother's deathbed* . . . . His heart surged up, a hammer under his ribcage. His mother's face, puffy and gray. His father's face, the anger in it. He had to get away, to escape, and *she* was still there. He could feel her presence behind the door. She was waiting on him. She had always been waiting. She would try to stop him. They had all tried. His father called. The echoes of his call seemed to spread out over the walls of the room. An urgency that would not be satisfied closed over him. He must get out. She was dying. Her voice called his name. He screamed, "I'm coming!", and started for the door. Stopped and backed away. Suddenly he was shaking. He felt he was drowning. His face twisted into a palsied look of terror; then his mind lost purchase and something broke free, disconnected and blank.

Slowly turning toward the corner of the room an edge of cunning exaggerated the look of surprise that had come over him. The solution. It had been there all the time. The gun. His hands fastened over it like gears coming together in a perfect fit. Pain crowded up under his chest. He threw open the door and his mind slipped again. He was remembering a kitten he had held as a child that had nuzzled against his neck and sucked at his ear.

#

A shotgun pointed into her breast she backed down the porch steps, her square-heeled patent leather shoes finding each step

33

with slow motion care. The hammer was cocked. His finger on the trigger. Still she did not speak, but her heavy-jowled sixty-year-old face had become rigid with anger. She backed onto the front lawn and he followed her, his eyes wide and unfocused, moving to her left. His breath came with quick sucking gasps. Sharp pain broke in his face. The gun tilted. Suddenly his eyes went empty, his face turned toward the sunlight falling through the gray. A bright green haze rose inside a yellow column of light.

V

Home

She woke and found the bed empty. Her sleep-heavy face clicked into wakefulness. She sat up, reached for her teeth, and slid from beneath the warm quilt. There was no feel of him anywhere in the house. He was gone. Wearily she made coffee while she dressed.

She found him in his rocking chair on the front porch. It had happened sometime during the night. He was dead. She spread a blanket over him, walked to the nearest farm for a telephone, and called Bud, their oldest. Papa rocked until they came for him.

THE PALACE OF NEW BEGINNINGS

Alison wanted to believe that words made no difference, but words were her weakness. She had agreed to see him.

She stared at the snow. The apartment grew cold. The couch suddenly became ugly, a brown that made no sense, wouldn't ever die out, a brown she watched spreading around her holding the room to the carpet. At first it was like drowning in air, a slipping inside oneself feeling the darkness close as though a zipper were being shut. But then like a wave leveling back into the body of a lake, her emotions retreated. The couch remained a thing of cushions and legs, a matter of ordinary experience. Outside it continued to snow.

Alison Benet was thirty-three. She had one child, David Benet, was now separated from her husband, John David Benet. It was midnight, but even so she decided to bathe and wash her hair. John would be coming tomorrow. She began to undress where she stood. The snow would not stick. Tomorrow would be a mess. Her body tingled from the chill on the room. Yes, she had grown thin. She lifted one breast and examined it, let it fall. Her body seemed a separate thing to her, something that lived, breathed, felt of its own will. It had not always been so. She had been young once. When? How long ago? She stared at the veins, just visible coursing blue tracks, her breast rising with her breathing. John would be coming. For an instant his large face on the pillow. She had been young once. Tomorrow he was coming. No, she did not hate him. All at once she wanted to laugh. Why had she agreed to see him? Because she needed to see him again, she thought, once more, know him, know his hands on her, know for the last time he meant nothing to her.

John David rises alone. It's early morning. The clatter of his dressing fills the cabin. Tennis shoes padding to a square kitchen sink. In a mirror the size of his hand he brushes his teeth, splashes water at his face. It's cold, ice cold. He smiles. His large face does not fit the mirror. Two rows of teeth, pieces of grinning cheek, open large nostrils bring him the morning.

Outside he begins to run. One lap of the lake. Three miles. It has taken him two months to build up to it. The right distance, he had decided, enough given, enough taken away. The cottonwoods around the lake loom up stark and pale out of the white morning. He crosses the ruins of a barbed wire fence, descends a small incline, and begins to run again. Soon the heavy snow will come., The lake will freeze over and his routine will be broken. But for now, again he settles into the pace. The muffled steps of his running lift into stillness.

A slow warmth spreads through his arms and legs. His glasses grow opaque in the cold. He knows this path. Barren, half-white trees lift over him dripping with snow. He runs, half-perceived images striking at the edges of his vision, and the outside world of lake, trees, and snow begins to slip away. He would be with her in a few hours. They had been separated almost three months now. Why did he want to see her again? Why had he talked her into it? He imagined her running naked before him in the snow. He wanted her. He couldn't help himself. In his mind he was chasing her, but she was like a bird, pretended she was hurt, leading him away from something, something she did not want him to find. And he followed her, her heavy blond hair over her back, laughing at him now, he wanted her, his breath coming faster, the way she danced, and suddenly he was running and she was afraid. He would take her now. She could not last and he was running flat out, he would have her, flat out into nothingness.

Where the path curved back to his cabin he came to a halt. Immediately he was cold. Overhead a shaftless arrow of ducks going South. Suddenly Alison was a reality again.

#

She placed two blouses on her bed—David had spent the night with his grandparents—and walked to the window wearing

36

jeans and sandals. Already the snow was melting. It remained piled only in shadows. The coffee pot began crackling on the stove. She poured herself a second cup, but did not drink any. Returned to her bedroom and rejected the Mexican print for the white silk. Then, before the mirror, tortoise-shell rose tinted glasses, peacock feather ear-rings, no bra, her blond hair tied in a loose braid, she thought it's not a matter of deception, but of pleasure. Why did it take me so lolng to discover that? She returned to her coffee, but it was cold. She poured it out, turned the burner on low, he would be arriving any minute now. She sat down to wait.

#

John David Benet roared to a stop before the florist's shop, raced the engine once and turned it off. For a moment he seemed a night rider, a vision of death and destruction. Off came his black mask, his rain suit glistening, and he ran inside to return with a dozen long stemmed roses. Then even the roar of his cycle seemed the expression of something gentle, a dream discovered to be reality, a simple man on a simple journey.

#

At the door to her apartment he suddenly became nervous. A presentiment. She would refuse him. In a rush he saw it all. She would be dressed up, the apartment clean, and David would be gone, staying with her parents again. It was a set up. She would refuse him. He looked down at his clothes. They seemed baggy and ill-formed. Behind the door she would be waiting, beautiful, waiting for him to try something, waiting to refuse him. He felt ridiculous. He wanted to put on his rain suit again, his helmet, rush through the door and attack her as she stood with her hand still stretched out to him. Suddenly he wanted to leave, sneak down the stairs, and leave. She would refuse him. That thought spinning around and around finally dropped inside him like an anchor. He felt it sinking, felt the line grow taut, and placing his motorcycle gear on the floor, lifting the roses before him, he knocked on the door. On hearing the rustle of her approach, a hot wave rushed at his face.

#

The roses in a blue vase between them, they seemed unable to find the right tact for conversation.

"How's David?", he said, and looked around the room as though expecting to find him hidden somewhere, his gaze finally coming to rest on a tiny racing car wedged under the credenza.

"He's fine," she said, "he wanted to spend the night with my parents." There was a tone of self-defense to her voice which she did not like.

He smiled, grimly.

And then, "You're looking beautiful today," without looking at her, the words like a challenge. And he could not look at her, her nipples clearly visible beneath the silk, noticed the racing car was missing a wheel, wanted to take down her hair, run his hands under her breasts, was grateful for the roses between them.

And she accepted the challenge. She *was* beautiful today. She knew it, knew it as a pleasure that tingled inside her, knew he could not look at her, knew it and reached forward, pushed the roses over to one side, said, "Well now, let me have a look at you."

HAMBURGERS

Billy Watkins
Bird Mill Road
Bogalusa, Miss.

Aug. 5, 1958,

Dear Billy,
   Just arrived here at the Grand Canyon. What a ditch! No, really a beautiful place, you should of come. Molly's standing over my shoulder here, says to tell you you are the sweetest brother-in-law a girl ever had and please remember to water the lawn and lock up. Bogalusa ain't the crime capital of the world, but you and I both know there's some will take anything not nailed down.
   Car did just fine—Molly says to tell you how Ma and the kids are having the most fun of their lives—actually they all been driving me nuts—stop here, look at that, let's all do this. But as I was saying the car's doing just great. Two quarts of oil is all so far and we been hitting 70 all the way. Told you you should have got a Ford when I did. Well, my hand's getting in a cramp from writing so much, see you when we get back,
                                        Luke.

Billy Watkins
Bird Mill Road
Bogalusa, Miss.

August 8, 1958,

Dear Billy,

I don't know how to go about saying this, but last night after
we climbed down to the bottom and back Ma went to bed real
early saying she was just wore out. Well, this morning when we
woke up we found that she had passed away during the night. So
now we are here at the Holiday Inn in Flagstaff and Ma is laid out
on the bed with us and I don't know what we are going to do.
God, I sure wish you had a telephone. I keep thinking about Ma.
The way she looked riding on top of that old mule, just holding
on for dear life. I guess we shouldn't of taken her with us. But she
sure wanted to see that Grand Canyon. Well, she saw it and that's
that.

Billy, you wouldn't believe what one guy told us on the
telephone about how much it costs to send a dead person from
Flagstaff to Bogalusa. $500.00 or more! I just don't know what we
are going to do. I thought maybe you could ask Hawkins and
those guys to try to scrape up some bucks to send to us cause I
know it's going to cost more than I got on me—I certainly don't
have no $500.00 anyway. So, I'm sending you this letter by
special delivery and hoping you will get it by tomorrow. I sure
hope you do cause I don't know what we're going to do and we
sure can't stay here much longer. Molly's going out of her mind
the way it is.

Write us and let us know about the money as soon as you're
able.

Luke.

Billy Watkins
Bird Mill Road
Boglusa, Miss.

August 10, 1958,

Dear Billy,

Just thought you'd like to know we couldn't wait no longer so
I took things into my own hands. It was a hell of a mess, but I've
got everything under control, everything but Molly that is. She
ain't done nothing but cry and tell me what a sacriledge I'm
making. Hell, there wasn't nothing else could be done. Those
people at the Holiday Inn were just getting to the point we
couldn't keep them out of our room no longer. So I've taken that
tarp, you remember the one I got from the mill, wrapped her up
in it and tied her to the top of the car. It was real funny though.
After I brought the tarp in I couldn't look at her no more. I just
had to turn my head. And then after I got her wrapped and water-
proofed and went to pick her up, it was like there wasn't anything
to her, like in dying all the weight had been taken out of her. Hell,
I couldn't even tell she was in there.

Anyway, we're planning to check out of this place in an hour
or so and then drive twenty hours a day until we get home.
Should be about day after tomorrow. So, I would appreciate it if
you would get the funeral all set up for the day after we get back.
I guess that'd be Thursday.

Luke.

p.s. Sorry we couldn't wait no longer for the money, but we just
had to do something. Billy, this is being real hard on all of us. I
sure hope you got things ready when we get there. Now, on top
of everything else it looks like it's going to rain.

Billy Watkins
Bird Mill Road
Bogalusa, Miss.

August 12, 1958,

Dear Billy,
There must be a curse on us Watkins. I don't know how else
to explain what's gone wrong. We drove all night last night and
by this afternoon when we hit Little Rock we seemed to have it
licked. We went through three rain storms and with all this heat,
Molly afraid she's smelling something all the way, and the kids
screaming that they're starving to death, we decided to stop and
rest for awhile. So, when we saw this big Hamburgers sign at that
truckstop right off the highway, we parked in the back and all of
us run inside without looking back once.

The car was just running great and I figured we could make it
home in under six hours the way things were going, so we just sat
there, none too anxious to go back to the car you understand, for
about two hours. And when we did, my God Billy, she was gone.
No sight of her anywhere, car and all. It was stolen Billy. Some
fucking bastard stole my car. So now we are here stranded at the
police station in Little Rock. Course I didn't tell them about Ma.
Just reported my car as stolen. But I keep wondering what those
bastards are going to do when they find what else they've stolen.
Billy, I been thinking about it, and I don't think we're ever going
to see her again. I think we had better just keep this whole thing
to ourselves and go on with a funeral service as if nothing at all is
the matter.

Anyway, the police here say they reckon we can hitch a ride
with a prison van going over to Sharkey tomorrow. We can wait
for you there, okay? We can figure out more of what to tell
people then.

Billy, it just keeps going over and over in my head, if only we
hadn't stopped for those goddam hamburgers. And I keep think-
ing of Ma sitting up there holding on to that long eared mule. I
just don't understand how so much could go wrong in such a
short time.

See you in Sharkey.

Luke.

APPLES

[from a novel in progress]

Up only two more flights. The rank smell of the stairwell
made him wince. The off-green walls peeled like a sun-burnt
corpse under a weak, almost brown light bulb. At the roof door
he stopped and looked down. He had always been fascinated by
long flights of stairs, like the one he had seen in Montgomery,
Alabama, the one that had no supports and wound mysteriously
toward the bedroom where Jefferson Davis had slept. He had been
ten then. The image of that incredible staircase polished to a deep
museum brown flickered briefly, and then faded from his mind.
From the back of his throat he coughed. He had not been able to
rid himself of the cold he had caught the very day he and Jeela
had arrived in New York. They had wandered about in a rain for
hours, unable to take it in, the streets of New York, unlike
anything they had expected. He thought of her again, their first
night in that cheap hotel, counting out on the bed their $600.00 in
twenties, the way she leaned against him, somehow already giving
up in the way she offered herself without looking at him. He
pushed her out of his thoughts, leaned over the banister and spit.
The snot and saliva fell wavering in an updraft that seemed to
hold it buoyant for two or three flights; then it plummeted and hit
with a good satisfying smack.

Clayton Morgan was not a large man. He had always hoped
for five foot ten but had settled finally for five seven. He stood
now at the top of the stairway and felt himself grow even smaller.
Like a small diminished man standing at the end of a long tunnel,
he looked down through the stairwell and waited for someone to
come out, to recognize him perhaps. But nothing moved. His
hands drifted over the smooth wood of the banister rail; its
smoothness seemed out of place with the dull lighting, the green

concrete walls that oozed a dampness out of long irregular cracks. He shook himself loose from the railing and turned toward the black iron door behind him.

Clay had swallowed a number of pain killers, Percodan, he didn't remember how many, and he was feeling rather quiet and sleepy as he pushed open the door. But once outside he felt wide awake. The cold night air rushed over him. He could feel the presence of the people and traffic on the street below. Avenue B. And then a burst of music, a solo jazz saxophone. Someone must have opened the door to the cafe down below, the Old Reliable. In his mind there came the feel of that small stage drifting under the smoke, the red flood lights, the odor of milling blacks, and for a while he simply stood and tried to listen to the music; but he couldn't follow the thread, and suddenly it ceased. In its absence he felt alone, separated.

In the black Clayton could feel the heavy clouds low over the city. As he sniffed the air he experienced his first doubt. It was going to rain. He could smell it. But then he smiled, almost laughed, and thought, what possible difference could it make? The tarred gravel roof was dark with close rectangulars. A maze of wires crossed over the spaces between the small closed shapes. Clay leaned over to avoid the wires and started across the roof. He was almost to the wall facing onto the street when he tripped and a sharp pain jabbed him just below his right knee. It was a capped metal pipe about a foot high. The pain flushed over him like warm water as he bent over and pulled up his pantleg. He couldn't tell if he was bleeding or not. He laughed loudly, "What the hell are pain killers for anyway?" But his voice disturbed him. It hadn't sounded like his and it had seemed so quickly swallowed up. He stood suddenly quiet and trembling. His first thought was to run, but he knew there was no place he could run to. "Where, little buddy?", he asked himself. And although something inside kept wanting to break and run, kept up a kind of feeling that said, this time it's different Clay, it's different, he had expected it, he granted it nothing. It was a feeling he had dealt with often enough, often enough.

He had thought about how it was going to be. For almost two weeks, almost from the day Jeela had left, he had thought of nothing else. Now the stubbornness that was his strength took possession of him. He refused to think of Jeela. Like everyone else, he had failed her. It was over. He swished his hand through

44

his loose, blond hair. Then, his jaws set, his fists clenched, he moved swiftly toward the chest-high parapet. It was like the fight in Birmingham, he thought, getting started was the hard part, you have to make up your mind and then just do it. He concentrated on the day of that fight. He had gone to the back lot of the A & P grocery knowing that his chances were not good. Clay remembered him: the name was Thompson, easily six-three, the way he had come out of the grocery removing his apron, how he had looked down on Clay, his greasy black hair combed straight back into a stiff duck. He was so sure of himself unclipping his bowtie, taking off his starched white work shirt, the way he laughed and handed over his three false front teeth, his reward for a spring vacation gang fight in Panama City, Florida. Under the lunch hour summer sun the dimes in his penny loafers glared up like extra eyes as Thompson went into his crouch, began dancing around and jabbing the air. Clay had stood in the center of the circle of onlookers and simply stared, his hands at his sides, as though he held this large and dangerous animal on the end of an invisible tether, watching with the fascination of one who already knew in advance what was about to happen, whose only interest seemed to be in when it would happen.

Clayton Morgan reached up and felt along the bridge of his nose. It was still slightly crooked from that first blow. His fingers were tingling, his nose felt strangely puffy and cold. Across the street on another roof top someone lit up a cigarette. Another suicide? The thought went through him and he laughed and knew he was in control of himself. It was the same way he had felt after Thompson had hit him, a strange sense of exhilaration taking over. And when a pigeon whirred to a perch not fifteen feet away he did not turn to look. His eyes had turned inwards on Thompson's face hovering over him, Thompson laughing with that hole in his face, laughing, his tongue touching the empty sockets and daring Clay, daring him to get up again. And up he came. And wiping the blood away they began again the circling, no longer testing but hitting out with all that was in them and hoping for the blood to show. And then that look on Thompson's face, the recognition that Clay would not stay down, that look of bewilderment edged with anxiety. And as Thompson turned to plead with someone to stop the fight before he had to kill Clay, Clay had rushed him swinging and felt his first solid blow catch Thompson in the throat, heard somewhere in the distance a terrible gasping for air, and felt Thompson's face going wet under his fists as many hands began dragging him away.

The pigeon suddenly throbbed with the sound of beating wings and Clay turned almost beginning to back away. A voice clamored once, this time it's different, and ceased. Clay stared and the bird, its smooth black head turning around, stared back. It seemed completely unafraid. A thread of jazz hit the air and died. Clay looked up toward the heavy clouds and said, as if to the bird, "Going to rain tonight."

Suddenly and again, loneliness swept over him and Clayton Morgan was afraid. He remembered Jeela's face, hauntingly empty, crazy. No, he thought, don't let it be this way, and he struggled against something that seemed to come from within. He held up his hands. They were shaking. "Come on, make a good ending of it," he said. He willed them to be still, and then reached into his back pocket and pulled out his wallet. He started to look through it, then changed his mind. There was no point to it. He flipped it over the wall and smiled at the thought of how long his wallet would remain unnoticed on the street below. Not long at all. Only a body now, a body with no identity found on a roof top in New York City. It was a comfort to him.

Now, he thought, now. He reached for the razor blade in his inside coat pocket. Touched it. It felt small and meaningless, more of paper and cardboard than steel. His fingers fumbled over the wrappings. It was the pain killers, he decided, they were making him feel tired, almost numb. And suddenly he knew that what had to be done must be done quickly. He felt he was losing control over his body. It was as though the darkness were jelling around him.

At the first touch of the blade, at the sting of its entrance, he closed his eyes and then pressed down hard. There was barely any pain at all. He opened his eyes and there it was between his finger and thumb, the blade half-buried into his wrist. Then almost as if another hand had come to steady his, he watched as from a great distance a stranger's hand begin the severing of his life. The wrist seared white and burst into a dark red that was more black than red. His left hand abruptly lost all sensation. The nerves, he thought, I've cut through the nerves, and stared down at his limp left hand. It just hung there, not his, attached to him somehow crookedly and wrong. Then unexpectedly, a problem of practical implications. With no left, how to sever the right? But his fingers

46

would not take hold and he dropped it. Enough, he thought, the left pumps well enough, all that's required.

Clayton leaned against the wall. He watched the blood welling up over his wrist, spread out over his arm and hand, a small trail down over his fingers. He remembered the floating staircase he had seen in Montgomery in Jeff Davis's home, that delicately balanced architectural feat whose strength depended on the placement of each step of the spiral around an invisible core. And that was what his life was like, Clayton thought, only something had gone wrong in the design somehow, one board misplaced, something off-center in the structure, something warped, and now the pieces were coming apart. He was ruined. He was beyond repair.

Clayton turned and looked out over the wall. Then he smiled weakly for himself. He still had a good right hand. He used it to light a cigarette. As his match popped against the rough cement he watched the pigeon stretch and prune one wing. For a moment he thought he saw touches of purple and then green. The match went out. The neon signs reflected up from the street. Everything appeared to stand still, the way it had been before he had come here, the way it would be when he was gone, a kind of hulking permanence that had always seemed to lie somewhere just beyond his grasp. Then, from the building top across the street, a lit cigarette began a high long arc out away from the building. And as it lost the grace of its momentum, the cigarette fell into the wind shedding sparks all the way to the street. Clay looked across to the other roof top. It remained dark. A slow helpless disquiet settled over him. It felt like something had gone wrong and he couldn't, didn't understand, and panic surged under his ribcage. He turned his back to the wall and began slipping down to a squatting position. He was cradling his left arm like a wounded child. The wrist, opened, the blood dripping warmly down his side. So much blood, he thought, all over me.

A sudden clear desire not to die swept over Clayton Morgan. It came with such strength that before he could stop himself his legs began to shake, and had he not already fallen to a sitting position he would have made a run for the door. Then, for several long moments he had wanted desperately another chance, not to die but to begin over again. He sat rigidly still. It was as though all the balance of his life had gone out of him, and he felt himself falling, like he was inside some huge floating structure that had

47

begun tilting in the dark. All his life it seemed he had been struggling against this feeling of falling. It was the same feeling he had known as a child when, before sleep, the world seemed to turn away from him, leaving him alone in his bed gripping the covers with both hands.

Slowly Clay returned to himself. He felt weak and shaken, but he could force himself to look at his wound, to accept the fact of what he had done, to be willing to let the future go on without him. He reached out, touched his flesh, his arm and hand, once sound and perfect in all its hidden connections. The blood felt sticky and warm, almost pulpy.

Then he began to feel sleepy and stood up. Something in him that did not want to sleep yet. A thread of jazz sounded very far away. Jeela's face rose in him unbidden. What if they'd never come to New York? Clay remembered that night beside Turkey Creek, the two of them naked, touching each other's body. She had been the first to touch him with her tongue, her eyes following his hands, his own tongue reaching inside and touching her, softly her thighs lifting and offering each taste, and never before had he known that sense of belonging so completely to another's touch. And later, the sudden feel of his desperation, his unwillingness to let her go when he saw her husband sitting in the upstair's window, waiting for her to come home.

Clay had wanted her the way a man wants something rare and fragile, not because he wants something back, but simply because she was there and seemed to call out to him to take her. She had had other affairs before him, but there was that difference about her. She had always remained innocent, untouched. She had told him once that her experiences with men never really happened to her, but to some other woman who was both her and yet not her. It was one of the many things Clay had never understood about Jeela. He struggled to reconstruct that night beside Turkey Creek, to keep out of him her face the day they took her back, that fragile child's face that had not recognized him, her blue eyes gone quiet and blank and sheared from any claim he could make on her. He remembered how they had laughed at the broken glass and beer cans they had had to clear away before placing the blanket down. Even then, that first night, she had seemed reaching out to find in him something he had been afraid he did not possess, some invisible core of strength in which she too could stand. And yet he had offered it as easily as he had taken her. He had promised he could save her. He had pulled her to him there on the ground. It was in him, he had promised himself, enough stubborn strength to make it work. He had wanted her and, it made no difference she was married, that people had said she was crazy, he would have her. He had known it for a long time, long before ever reaching the point of speaking to her. And on that night, even in all the garbage surrounding them, they had discovered what he had felt all along. And they had made love believing they owned each other—she would be safe with him. In his mind Clay could hear the soft pine popping in the fire, the sound of a beer can trapped against a rock, the creek water purling and breaking downstream.

Jeela's face rises in him now and he sees her as she had stood before him, waiting for him to accept her gaze, her eyes seeking him out, asking if he will accept the offering she is making of herself; and as he looks, a shadow seems to draw over her face; her gaze no longer greets his, not asking or waiting, not even recognizing him, but turning backwards toward some other time and place where he does not exist, security no longer needed, not even asked for, her blue eyes empty and trapped smiling inside some different kind of dream. Broken. Crazy.

The sudden drumming of wings seemed to come from within until Clay turned, knew that the pigeon had taken flight, and saw a man coming out of the door with a flashlight in his hand. He was searching for something. Clay stood up and stared as the stranger crunched across the gravel in his direction. The light wandered nearer and nearer until it settled on his shoes, stopped, and then moved up. There was a blinding light in his face. Clay instinctively lifted his hands to cover his eyes. The two of them stood in silence, the light holding them locked together in a kind of mutual discovery of something overwhelming and beyond the boundaries of words or movement. For long moments they stood just so, but then Clay felt himself beginning to crumble beneath the light. His arms grew too heavy to hold up in front of him. His back began to ache, his legs were shaking, his head throbbing from some deep and inward heaviness, and he stumbled toward the light with a suddenness that meant he was falling . . . . Then the light was gone and Clay, who had somehow managed to stay on his feet, watched, from his awkward and stumbling posture, the light squeezed tighter and tighter around the edges of the door until at last the dark had sealed it shut.

Clay knew that he had passed out when he lifted his head, remembered where he was, and realized that he was the reason for the sirens and the growing intensity of noises coming from the street. It was then he thought of the stairwell. He struggled to his feet and moved across to the door. But once there his hand stuck to the doorknob, and he could not get it open. It was as though some inhuman strength held it closed against him. And when he finally did get it opened, and staggered inside, he felt he had crossed some dimensional barrier. He knew this place. Everything seemed to wait for him merely to step forward to complete what had already happened in some distant past. He realized the stairwell, not as though he were alive and standing above it, but as a memory, as something he had already lived through. And then the memory faded. The world became real again. He found he was having trouble standing. He heard them running on the stairs. He pulled himself up by the banister rail; but once up, everything began to spin. He knew that he was falling: he felt himself turning around and over, upside down, the stairs falling away, the steps collapsing above him, falling and splintering, a deep mahogany brown whirling over him suddenly spinning outwards rushing toward a blackness, a mouth opening with three teeth missing, a black pigeon flying out of it, shedding sparks, a deeply familiar woman's face abruptly emptying into a shotgun blast, and blood red pellets streaking time lapsed and bending, becoming a long blinding column of light . . . .

#

A sense of weightlessness hovers over him, that and a dryness in the back of his throat. He feels a need to swallow, but can not. For some time he lies there, breathing, feeling his body come back back to him. His right hip and leg ache, but it is a pain that moves slowly about the edges of his consciousness. A desire to roll over on his side, but he does not try.

Suddenly Clayton Morgan realizes that he is alive and that he is in an ambulance. He feels vaguely aware of the two attendants up front, white coated men talking and smoking. A siren wails loud and meaningless, waves that crash over him in one long continuous shock.

Then he notices the thin rubber tubing attached to his arm. It is not over. Pull the plug, he thinks, pull the plug and let it be over, his right hand fumbling but closing around the tubing, the rip of tape, the needle sliding under the body, the slow warmth collecting around him, over, let it be over, all sensation leaving him, a slow film of brown covering everything.

#

He has not yet opened his eyes for there is, within him, like the conscious sleep of one who knows that the morning has already begun without him, a deep inward pool of darkness that warms and holds him. He does not know where he is and he does not care. He feels inside an ever widening peacefulness, and everything is as it was, and as it should be. He begins to hear for the first time the rain striking softly against a window pane somewhere behind him. As he listens to it he imagines he can smell the wetness in the air, and then suddenly he is awake.

The room is so white he, at first, takes it to be a dream. But he knows that it is not. His eyes turn slowly toward a large bottle of plasma. It drips through a long brown tube that ends in his arm. Then he notices the cast on his leg, the restraints binding his arms, the thick mound of bandages across his left wrist. He stares down the length of himself, bound, and feels himself wanting to float upwards. He feels his body has no weight. It is as though the restraints are being used to keep him from lifting from the bed. The sound of the rain gusting against the window fills his consciousness. The ache in his leg and hip is almost a comfort to him; it crosses through him like distant waves, touching his mind and then receding, something heavy with substance that rises and falls and holds him stable against his weightlessness.

He closes his eyes and in his mind he is riding a loud metal-wheeled hay wagon. He is on his back on the top of the pitched load. He does not hear the nurse when she enters and begins checking over his chart. She is a student nurse who has just come on duty. As she reads over his chart, her eyes glance toward her patient with a warmth and a concern that has a lightness about it. She realizes that he is conscious and begins to take his pulse, and then to check his blood pressure. Clay opens his eyes at her touch, but he does not see her. In his mind he is still on the hay wagon and he has seen that he is going to pass beneath the upper limbs of an apple tree. But though he has begun to reach for the apples, he is beginning to lose the vividness of his memory; and the nurse is moving in, her words coming out of nowhere.

She speaks, gently,

"You're lucky you know . . . your veins collapsed."

And he nods as he reaches for an overburdened limb that is moving beyond his grasp; and no sooner has he taken hold of it than the wagon has moved on, the limb pulling at him, his fingers seeming unwilling to function, to take hold of even one of them, and a voice, insisting, insisting that he answer,

"What's your name?"

"Apples . . . ."

And he had one, the voice again, doubting, insistent for a response,

"What's your name?"

"Apples . . . ."

And suddenly he has grown quiet, his eyes smiling, then closing, and he moves on toward the barn and into sleep.

The young nurse watches over him. She reaches down, pulls the top sheet up across his chest, and tucks it tightly under his mattress. She moves around his bed and takes up his chart again. After recording the results of her examination she hesitates. His face is smooth, an air of peace in his quiet breathing. She makes one last entry on the chart and backs to the door. The sleeping form drifts. The rain continues its slow drumming against the window pane.